SEASONS AND CELEBRATIONS

A Collection of Poems

by

BARBARA NOEL SCOTT

To the memory of my beloved teacher
Elizabeth Garratt
1894 - 1962

ENVOI POETS PUBLICATIONS, PEN FFORDD, NEWPORT, DYFED, SA42 0QT, WALES, UK

Previous publications
The Wild Poppies
Island Voices
Music in Another Room

ISBN 1 874161 17 8

Some of the poems have appeared in OUTPOSTS, ENVOI,
ENVOI Summer Anthology 1991, CHRISTIAN POETRY 1976,
THE BRIDGE, etc.

British Library Cataloguing-in-Publication Data.
A catalogue record for this book is available from the British Library.

ENVOI POETS PUBLICATIONS

AUBADE

Summer comes late
to my cold house.

At five, it's light
a white page
scribbled with birdsong

Their notes are clusters
little flower shapes
pressed on pale silk
as though with finger tips

veils transparencies
infinite fields of light
scattered with unknown flora

dawn-lit my swaying
curtains show their flowers.

My house is bare
swept, full of emptiness.
Summer is late
the dawn is not too early.

CLOUDED MAY

Green, green
under thick folds of grey
thinned to an eye of pearl
the sheen
shimmer and swirl
of grass blown all one way
a soft remembrance where the sun has been
light scent of cow parsley
the breath of May.

Innumerable veils one over one
as through shut eyes, diffuse
this delicate light
rayless and shadowless
so little bright
and yet enough to use
filling the room between me and the sun.

Nothing I want that is not far away
lost, or long vainly sought.
And yet, today
brushed with this transient light
the drift and flow
of wind in grasses, I receive the thought
that all I want is nothing
but as though
nothing were everything
this clouded May.

SEEING AND SAYING

The air is cold, clear of doubt,
a day cut with diamond.
Softer days do not have this
brilliant definition
the veins of leaves
jewel of a drake's head
the sharp fracture of water.
Vision cuts through the wrapped sense
wanting warmth, fragrance, lethargy
shivers thin ice
disturbing a new perception.

How can I tell of these things?
If I could carve the whole day
out of a single piece of jade
or paint it leaf by leaf
inside a crystal globe
the hardness, if it were possible at all
might give precision to the meaning.
But how with blunted words
pare out this narrow essence?
Words in themselves are worthless,
they tell you only
what you already know.

A LILY

All night while I slept
she has stood here awake,
the room has the scent
of her breathing.

I am aware of a presence
still, yet charged —
there is movement in such stillness
the spread and fill of sails
in crisped back petals,
suffusion of pale veins,
the wave-line where the edge turns over.

Nearness perceives vibrations of
poised attention
a listening
also a silent song.
She is an ear, a throat
a living trumpet offered to the air
breath for her breath.
Some music passes through her
that flows, lifts, holding her
perfectly open.

She cannot go back on this.
A lily's life is too short
for sleep.

THE WINTER GARDEN

Dense, sodden pulp-paper
sky, blots up daylight
holds the late noon
in suspension. Wet charcoal
has smudged-in the tree-lines
the branches of winter-
sweet flowering viburnum
and Japanese cherry,
snowberry, smoke-tree,
the orange and raspberry
cups of the spindle,
Siberian crab-apple
red as dark roses —
all hang such thin screens over
nothing, exposing
treasures of leaflessness,
scatters and tuftings
of berries, of blossoms,
white, coral, crimson,
while caught up in angles
or dangling from stem-tips
a shower, an amazement
of bright drops entangled
uplifted and waiting
like fruit, to be shaken.

SNOWFALL

Fresh snow
new dropped like flowers
bunching the bough
soft handfuls
of scarcely solid stuff
a wreath of air
gathered from far
cold space
caught million crystals
lodged where they touch
reluctant if at all
to mass and cling
slow drifting
drifting down
the heavy sky
as though surprised to fall.

END OF SPRING

May is fallen —
spires, towers
veiled sky cities
fallen in showers.

Mirage of white and rose
cloud in a glass —
fallen, dissolving,
pooled on grass.

Green jade the carved year
petals all blown
hangs, a green fruit,
a living stone.

LIGHT IN DECEMBER

To-day, the Sunday streets
dove-lit, grey silver
are cleared for the wind
to blow through.
The gardens are open
a gateway on ordered creation,
the sky a clear window
for the sun's will.
A space prepared, look!
Even the shortest day
this day in late December
gleams from the grass
perfect diamond.
Out of spent summers
numbered as they are
green winter springs.
There is no light but now.

GRASMERE CHURCHYARD

A path between the graves, vivid with grass,
clusters of snowdrops and small daffodils
lifting, nodding again as storm showers pass,
under slate-coloured yews, and darker hills.
Winding, it leads me to the stone I seek,
severe, without comment — simply name and date —
William and Mary Wordsworth. It seems to speak
of thought suspended, idly, now too late,
a book left open, under a yew-tree's shade.
He might have seen it so.
                          And now, a beam
breaking the edge of silvery cloud, has made
a rainbow. Ah! the visionary gleam
might come again! How well he might have caught
in one pure phrase, this moment, and this thought!

A VIEW OF TINTERN ABBEY

I turn a corner — suddenly, there it stands.
A wraith-like building, poised in misty light
from the deep-wooded, river-channelled gorge.
High though it is, the slopes of plunging green
and steep rock overtower it
yet cannot make it less — heighten the strangeness
of this appearance, in this place — a presence
archaic, solitary
lifting intense and delicately pointed
arches to meet, like supplicating hands.

Walk round it slowly, letting it speak at will
and only of itself. No history
intrudes upon the pierced, attenuated
form, that opens ever more profound
vistas of inward space, shot through
with wildness. Something hollow, yet complete,
worn thin, almost translucent, like a shell
washed with the oceans of long time, and raised
into another meaning. Look —
where those high windows, empty of all but light
drink in the green of trees, the blue of sky
indifferently, consenting to be still.

A BALCONY OVER THE SUSSEX WEALD

I lean, as martins do
from a high nest,
summer spread out below me — rivered plain
green to the cloud's blue hem —
soft cirrus foldings
float on a southward breeze.
Downsweep of lawns
the flare of flowers
then trees
chestnut and beech embank the eye
follow the involutions of the wind
in their loose robes.
While over and around me
wind-shaped, flint-coloured
quick as sparks
the martins flash
piercing the gulf of air
with flakes of light and dark.
Invisible windings
make visible the space where I look down,
the dizzy fall they circle endlessly
defining as they draw it.
Distances
are deepened yet brought near.
Wind, bird and cloud
are gathered in one stream.
And so am I.

SPRING HOLIDAY

for L.H.

Early March sun
pours primrose pale
honey on Cotswold
stone, heaped hills
rounded and pale
with houses in their laps
clustered like lambs.
The woods are lit
more gold than green
with their first flowering — hazel
willow and ash,
a lambency of pollen,
with here and there
the poplar's flamy rose,
and then the scattered
whiteness of thrown spray
wave-break of blackthorn's
leafless miracle.
A mist of colour
muted as a pearl.
You hand in hand with me
old amity
but tipped with new delight,
as there before us
the million million
brush points of the Spring
leap from a canvas
woven of dark boughs
winter and loss
and all the tears of things.

THE BAY TREE
Laurus nobilis

Laurel — a word
the wind tongues
over, in a dark dream.
A tree shaped like a leaf
veined to a dark core,
a steady flame
standing, breeze-blown
a little, never far from stillness.
Spire of innumerable
small flames brushed featherwise
into one flame
one darkness
a torch of night the wind endlessly
stirs but cannot quench.

INTEGRITY

Winter roots
rigid with frost
remain
when leaves are lost

lightless
unseen
they do not need
to be green

impelled to grow
deep
before buds
can show

too deep
to see
they yet contain
the tree

ESTUARY

Once again, the red sun-wreck
black marshes
ebb to the sea
a last ribbon of water
a strand of swans.
Once more
obedient to the hour
I leave you
leave the white house
window on estuary
where you and I touch hands
across our worlds
and in our words embrace.
I think I love you.
The sadness of the place
has told me this
exposing in my heart such wilderness
dragging my wrenched roots waterwards
once more.

2

Greyness, colour of waiting.
Cloud, marsh, silted weed
spread out like drying nets,
pasture for gulls.
Boats, grounded, rest aslant
on quilts of mud
seamed with salt rivulets,
sails shrouded, furled,
brown chrysalids
dreaming of wings.
Things earthbound need
another element.
Here, between ebb and flood
with melancholy thirst unsatisfied
everything waits
upon the turn of tide.

3

Full water
zenith of a day
mist-blue
waves lift against the breast of swans
turned tidewards
tender to the swell.
Sails red as poppies, white as wings
stand with their tall reflections.
Children play.

I saw two swans rise breast to breast
in delicate encounter
wings outspread
beak curved to beak in duel
they caressed.

Brown reedscum crusts the little beach
white floating feathers scooped like flowers.
Memories
ours.

MAKING FRIENDS

Heir of anxiety
orphan out of Europe
your hesitancy mars
only your male sureness.
To me, it is what speaks.
Sensitive plant, your stem of hurt
still feeds each shrinking leaf
with reflex evasions.
I, for once the hardier,
touch, tremble, wait
for the next unfolding,
troubled for you, not me.
A woman can respect tender things,
feeling behind the shy apology
a barbed strength
delicately sheathed.

A LITTLE GIRL

Small cat-face, callow, wise,
round cheeks, pointed chin
eyes largely spectacled
above the button nose,
lips a prim bud
pink pout or pearly laughter.
Soft silk of hair —
I swathe it in my hand —
kitten or gosling down
could not be softer.

Spruce greenstick limbs
poised for the leap, the flight,
spilikin-balanced
on tip-tilted toe,
as topmost tender twig
limber and light
caught in the wind's
impatient to and fro.

Alert as some small beast
or bud, or bird
things downy, delicate, and quick,
an innocence
a valiant tininess
slips through my hand
then turns for a caress
leaving a freshness
printed on my cheek.

VISIT TO A SON IN ANN ARBOR, MICHIGAN

A house built for the sun, white, weather-boarded
verandah-fronted, windowed deep, where trees
survivors from a mute arboreal age
carry a breath of wildness to our door
and lean their shade upon a sultry breeze.

My northern child, from our grey-skirted island
travelled in ways that I have never known
I visit, in this land of lakes and forests
christened the New World once, as though disclaiming
the continent from which that world had grown.

New to me still, this fierce and foreign sunlight,
this language, bent into a foreign tongue,
and new our meeting, fresh from being parted;
but old the mother-rock of understanding,
the echoing chant of waters ever young.

Far from the country of my own beginning
I am the child now, orphan'd of my past,
stripped by my searing passage through the air,
and come to rest with you, as birds migrating
home-in to their new feeding grounds at last.

Which is the mother-land between us two?
Across the distances from soul to soul
there is no path but must be blazed anew,
no space but to explore, no time but ours —
and everything we are to be made whole.

COLOURS OF DARKNESS

For a friend going blind

Light was her element
her language, colour.
Born to a brilliant sun —
white walls, black shadow,
hot sands, macaw-striped
dresses, fiery flowers —
her narrowed eyes
had learned to sift the blaze
for subtler, softer shades —
stones, grasses, grain of wood,
earth-painted pottery,
woven earth-dyes.

Now, in the colder country
of her exile,
cool colours rest her eyes —
the autumn garden
aster and rose
the willow-green of water
lit with the snowy drift of swans
drop comfort on her failing sight.
But now, behind those lids
where darkness falls
break the mysterious colours of a dawn
as yet unknown,
the archetypal light.

HONOUR TO THE DYING

for C.A.A.H.

Six foot and more of man laid on a bed.
A tree, whose branches reached the morning light
may thus lie prostrate on the forest floor
the foot brought level with the mighty head.
I gaze direct into his shadowed sight
closer to mine than I have known before.

Closer the fallen look, the troubled brow
bewildered by this sudden change of view
from high to low. A strong man in his prime
the hidden canker felled, lies tender now
to touch of pity, tremulous and new
that has not felt the withering hand of time.

A man of power, a kind and courteous man
he had the soaring patience of a tree,
the strength that others lean on, having known
himself the needs of shyness — one who can
by his own diffidence set others free,
conquer their fears by conquering his own.

No pride forbids compassion, for the wise
are humble, and accept it as they gave.
Where kindness is known currency, we dare
to take the hand, to look into the eyes,
receive the darkness, though we cannot save.
If any comfort is, we find it there.

DEMOLITION

The street's the same, familiarly rewarding
one of a hundred sentimental journeys,
but where the house stood, nothing ....
A space of sky, the shock of emptiness,
a great bole of my life sawn away.
Site for three town-type houses, the men tell me,
three storeys each with integral garage,
hard-standing for three cars.
Bricks, mortar-rubble, dust in the air.
No blade of green where the small orchard was,
the flower garden, the pillar rose,
bird-pool and arbour — gone, all gone,
tea on the lawn, the tray of lace and china,
the drift of lavendar in rooms,
the balcony for sleeping under stars.
Loves and rebellions, cherishings, tears.
Years piled on years, now silently fall.
My mother smiles from a vanished door.

A GIFT FROM NEW ZEALAND

A day of winter streets
wept ceaselessly — until
your book dropped through my door
stamped with your love
fresh from its swallow-flight
round half the world.
An open page of summer
suddenly bloomed
as joy found foothold in
dark slopes of pain
rock growing warm
with subterranean springs,
mountains of loss
with unexpected flowers.
Earth's Yin and Yang
eternally embracing.

RAINBOW

Rain bow
sun bow
delicate truce
hung drops
a fountain-fall of light
caight in suspension
over cliffs of thunder
pure arc of iris colours
rayed to the eye
a grace to all
to each a single wonder.

WINTER ROSEBUD

The small pink rose
tenderly shows
in the freezing air
like bare
flesh between the rents
of Winter's clothes.

And I, so old
withered but still aware
am also there
a sentience
exposed
and standing in the cold.

DISTANCES

For a son in New Zealand

Today I can't write.
It should be easy
to float off a line
to you in your far island.
Today, my hand can't lift
the weight of distance,
the pen (once called a plume)
refuses to take wing,
the air-blue letterform lies folded
flightless on my desk.
Swallows on telegraph wires
or messages in bottles
start with more faith
on comparable journeys.
I strain my eyes
till I am lost in blue.
Fathom-deep oceans
unscaleable mountains, divide us.

No, I can't reach you.
Distance unfolds
in the wingbeats of night and day,
in the vast alternations
of winter and summer
that lap the revolving globe.
I call — you are turned away in sleep
but when I sleep, you wake.
I am in yesterday, from where you are.
Seasons like generations roll between us.
You are my hostage to the scattering winds.
My seed floats over waters
in atoms of light.

Yet, deep in here and now
I find you are.
What distance can sever
that bond, that enfoldment
of each in the other,
the once that is always,
the milk of our sharing?
The substance, the shape of the sphere
is in brightness and shadow
uniting the poles
in a clasp of invisible hands.
So here, in the heart
is the presence
that absence affirms
that emptiness knows
as a wholeness that cannot be lost.

ASPIRATION

Mountain, you crack my heart
climbing the blue
with such serener purpose, purer art
than I climb you.

Feet heavy as stones
like an old cart, I press
my weight against your side with groans
of helplessness.

My gravity, my will
beyond — how far —
you mount forever, and are still
forever where you are.

FINALITIES

The low sun burns without heat
corrodes the sky's metal
a cold indecision shakes the thorn.
The wind keens
though it is April
the wind has swallowed spring
torn off green branches
thrown away blossoms.
The time of promise is sometimes bitter
despoiling what it gives.
Yet there are winters
that linger with a green solicitude.

After long silence
if I should speak
I tell what life has written.
There is a sadness in all seasons
a margin of unfulfilment.
The slender hopes
of daffodils or the last flush of rosebuds
caught by late snow or early frost
perversely entrench melancholy
the threat of loss, the sense of being denied.
But seasons are a language for the living.
The old have no quarrel with time.
Renewal is not spring, nor autumn harvest
to one who has already lived so long.

I cannot speak of time.
There are moments of seeing,
points of light
on waters moving darkly.
I do not know their meaning
but that they have the signature of wholeness
that they are chosen
singled out and shown me
lifted from pools like pearls
streaming silver
to rest in my hand.
The perfect round white stone
thrown on the shore.

LETTER TO A DISTANT FRIEND

Last night, you came to me in a rare dream.
Pale, as you always were, thinner — I felt the bones
fragile in my embrace. You did not speak
but I knew you as real. The white rose of your presence
wafted to me across oceans, recalling
afternoons in the garden at Henfield,
precious meetings, oases of comfort
in an unhappy world. Friend, counsellor, sharer
of sorrows, partaker in souls' communion,
I knew you again with something more than love.

Were you aware that we met? Did you dream, or imagine
my presence, to wake me from sleep with a thought?
Was it a missive, a true emanation
reaching me here direct from wherever you are?
Or was it a mask, an illusion, similitude out of the past
lighted upon sometimes as I wander in dreams
through the mind's deserted rooms? We cannot be certain
what such things mean; although they are not more strange
than the mystery of friendship, after all.

Useless to call on the past. The forests of Victoria
from where your pale infrequent letters come
are not more distant than that summer garden
relict of memory, a nest in time
from which the bird has flown. No easy solace
can salve that wound. To surmount separation
we cannot deny the reality of loss
lest we deny the true experience
that went before. The inestimable gift
of human love measures its weight in tears.

Mary, you are never distant from my heart
though continents divide us. There are meetings
that cannot be negated, deep exchanges
we carry still, a portion of all our becoming;
and by such strands we are inwoven with the world,
mingled in the timeless patterns of renewal
changing it, and ourselves. We celebrate
with all that we now are, the mutuality of being,
the alchemy of love, ever transmuting
our baser lives to gold, our griefs to wisdom.

A READING OF LIFE

Back in the place I came from, after all;
this modest suburb of the ancient city —
brick dollshouses in sampler-squares of garden —
nurtures my age. Rebellious daughter once,
I have come full circle, drawn by circumstance
that sometimes fits our need more than we know.
As a seed finds its own unlikely place
in walls and crannies, and there flourishes,
I rooted here. I look for no great changes.
I keep house, cultivate my garden,
watch for the first crocus, the yellow butterfly,
the late rose. Sit in the window
where the sun is, or rest in summer shade,
turning the pages of an unfinished life
scored with regrets. Too late now to rewrite,
too soon to throw away. Regrets stay green;
the bitter fruits of learning from them, ripen
to inky blackness, and perhaps grow sweet
only with death. We can keep nothing
but what we gave, that is certain.

Trees blur the limits of my tended garden,
filter the sun to chequered solitude
within a maze of gardens, fenced and shaded,
small kingdoms, smaller worlds. Families flower
in these small plots, and spend themselves in seed,
while the dried seed-heads wither on the stem
finding completion here. So little changes
in this quiet milieu, neither high nor low,
like my remembered home. It tempts me back
to recreate the green space of my childhood
perhaps to find a place I never knew.

Often, in summer, I wake before the dawn
and hear the first soft fluting of the birds
scatter cool drops out of the font of darkness.
Language of innocence before the cockcrow,
before the fall, baptising life anew.
Earlier than words, further than memory
that imprint lies. The ear within the ear
is touched and startled into recollection,
and knows again the white dawn of the world.

For innocence — if there be such a state
beyond our colder meaning of "illusion" —
is nowhere but perhaps in that first garden
where a child walks between the banks of flowers
along dim paths of dew, grows small with distance
towards a point where memories converge,
thought dwindles, dies into a pure sensation
naked, intense and sinless, which was joy.

Swifts with their silver shrieking milk the air,
they never touch the ground, mate on the wing,
drink distance with their scything wings. The bee
bends with his weight the delicate flower
sucking her dry in honey-thieving rapture.
Fat blackbirds in the amalanchier branches
strip the green fruit, and never let it ripen.
Innocent plunder. Such was the greed of youth,
wildness and waste; yet carelessly bestowing
out of experience, time's wealth,
the harvest of its own necessity.
There is a paradox that still lies hidden,
obscured with cloud, seen in elusive glimpses,
then for a moment opens like a koan.
"If I had known" — but knowing has its seasons.
The Sybil's leaves, bought from a past rejection
are now so few, can they contain the answer?

No power can restore the tattered pages
lost or defaced, or thrown away unopened.
But in the history of imperfect loves
some themes can be discerned, that may outlast
the errors of too much, or not enough,
too early, or too late — that painful legend.
The ring of friendship deeply marks the finger
faithfully worn, long after deaths and partings.
Sons borne and relinquished with pain, poems
burned from the heart's ore, go from us like blessings,
pure-minted currency, to the world's ends,
and our lost loves are worn like crowns of stars.
Giving, receiving, making and destroying
are mingled in the substance of our living
and feed each other endlessly. It may be
that imperfection is a part of wholeness,
that meaning rests with no recording angel,
nor any blotted catalogue of failures,
but here and now, in this suburban garden
where an old woman listens to the birds.

LATE DAYS

I do not remember a blue so fierce, so splendid
as now, in autumn, when the sun comes late
sweeping huge clouds from his path, and a half-moon floats
high up, a feather in celestial balance
in a sky grown infinite.
Such mornings! Were they ever? ever the high
serene mastery of those beams
that only refrain from burning, so they can touch
more gently now, with the warmth of a welcome hand.
Are we ever aware enough? Do we ever answer
or understand as we might, what is offered again
just when our life sinks low, and a dull resistance
cowers in us, telling us all is over — there
there is the summons, this blueness, the searing light
from the heart of a sapphire, the rim of the great sky's bowl
upturned in benediction, the absolute gift,
the gold-filled reassurance of the harvesting sun.